Crayons, Classmates, and Christ
Copyright © 2025 by Jude and John Publishing
Authored by Lakeisha Little.
All rights reserved.

No part of this publication may be reproduced, stored in a retrieval system, or transmitted in any form or by any means (electronic, mechanical, photocopying, recording, or otherwise) without prior written permission of the publisher, except in the case of brief quotations in reviews, articles, or as permitted by U.S. copyright law.

ISBN: 979-8-9931916-1-4

For more information visit
www.JudeAndJohn.com

Printed in U.S.A.

It was Show and Tell Day at Gingersnap Community School. The hallways buzzed with excitement. Everyone had something to show.

Colton's robot blinked and beeped. Priya opened a velvet box with her grandma's shiny necklace inside. Mateo proudly held up his soccer photo. Even Clara grinned as glitter sprinkled off her giant pinecone.

Eden smiled, but a tiny flutter of nerves danced in her stomach. What she brought wasn't shiny or loud, but it was something special. She wondered if she made the right choice.

She had thought about bringing her puppy, Mr. Bacon. But yesterday he tracked muddy paw prints all over the floor and made Mom upset.

Eden loved Mr. Bacon. He was adorable but wild. She knew her classmates would enjoy him, but Mom had said, "No more school visits until he learns to walk like a gentleman!"

She also thought about bringing her guinea pig, Snowball, but Snowball was in big trouble. Last night, she escaped her cage, waddled across the table, and nibbled right through Dad's dinner.

Dad left the room for one minute and came back to find a very guilty fluff ball sitting on his plate. Now Snowball was grounded, and Dad said, "No more gourmet guinea pig feasts!"

When Mrs. Jenson called her name, Eden took a deep breath. She didn't have a box or toy in her hands, but her heart felt full.

She stood tall in front of the class.

"Okay everyone," she said with a bright smile. "I don't have anything to show you today, but I do have something really big to tell you! It's the best story ever. It's about God's Son. His name is Jesus."

Eden continued, "Jesus was there when the world was made. He's older than everybody. Even older than Mrs. Jensen's grandma!"

The whole class burst into giggles.

One of Eden's classmates gasped and said, "No way that's true!" Another whispered, "Is that even possible?"

Mrs. Jensen laughed and nodded her head with a smile. "It's true ladies and gentlemen," Mrs. Jenson said.

"See, it's true!" Eden nodded excitedly. "Jesus has always been around. Before mountains, before animals, before cookies were even invented!"

Someone in the back gasped. "Before cookies!?"

"Yes!" Eden said with a smile. "And He made everything. Even cookies."

"Wait, even chocolate chip?!" one boy yelled.

"AND oatmeal raisin," Eden nodded. "Even though I think He knew we would all like chocolate chip better."

Now the whole class was listening.

"So, here's the story. The world was a big mess. People kept doing wrong things and forgot how to love God and each other. Their hearts needed help, and only Jesus could fix them. So, God sent His Son Jesus to help us.

But God didn't send Jesus as a superhero or a king with a shiny crown. God sent Him as a tiny baby, with little toes and squishy cheeks. He cried, needed milk, and learned to walk, just like you and me."

"His mother's name was Mary," Eden said. "But she didn't have a husband yet. God's Holy Spirit made the baby grow inside her.

It was a miracle! Like God put Himself in a people-suit!"

Eden paused, grinning. "Kind of like Mr. George at the school fair!"

The class giggled remembering Mr. George in the fox suit.

"Jesus grew up and never did one bad thing," Eden continued, stretching her arms wide. "Not even one! He never tattled just to get someone in trouble. He never told a single lie. He didn't whine or throw a fit when He didn't get His way. He didn't even roll His eyes when someone was mean."

The class gasped.

"Not even at siblings?" someone whispered. "Not even at siblings," Eden confirmed with a serious nod.

"He was perfect," Eden said. "But not the annoying kind of perfect. He didn't brag or act like a know-it-all. He was kind. He helped people. He listened. He was patient, even with people who were really hard to be patient with!"

Mrs. Jensen raised an eyebrow. "Sounds like someone who'd get a lot of gold stars."

"Totally!" Eden said with a smile.

"And guess what!" Eden said. "He was so smart that the teachers were amazed by how much He understood. He even helped some of the teachers understand things they got wrong!"

"No way!" said a classmate.

"You better believe it!," Eden said, nodding. "He asked big questions and gave even bigger answers. The teachers couldn't believe He already knew everything about God's Word."

Some of Eden's classmates were so shocked, they stared at her in disbelief.

"When Jesus grew up, He walked from town to town helping people," Eden went on. "If someone couldn't hear, He made their ears work. If someone couldn't see, He made their eyes work again. If someone couldn't walk, He told their legs, 'Get up!' and they did!

He made sick people feel better, told bad spirits to go away, and even brought people back to life!"

"One time, Jesus fed hungry bellies with just five loaves of bread and two little fish," Eden said. "Thousands of people ate until they were full, and there were even leftovers!

But Jesus didn't just fill tummies," she continued softly. "He made sad hearts feel happy again. When people felt worried or hurt inside, He spoke calm words that made them feel safe. He helped people start fresh when they'd done wrong, gave them hope, and told everyone how much God loves them."

"One day, a storm came crashing in.
BOOM! CRASH! SPLASH!
Big waves jumped around, thunder roared, and the boat rocked back and forth!

Jesus' friends were scared, but Jesus stood up and said to the storm, "Be still!"

And guess what? The storm listened.
The wind stopped, the waves sat down, and everything became calm because Jesus has power over the wind and the sea.

Even the weather listened to Him, because even nature knows He's God's Son!"

"Could He stop a snow day?" someone asked.

"Probably," Eden said. "But I think He'd let us sled first."

"Some people didn't like Him though. They didn't believe He was God's Son. So they were mean to Him. Like, super mean."

"Like worse than playground bullies?" a girl asked quietly.

"Way worse," Eden said softly, her voice becoming quiet. "They put Him on a cross to die."

"But you know what?" Eden said softly. "That was the plan all along! Jesus didn't even fight back. He chose to die. He didn't run or hide. He didn't call angels to stop it. He stayed because He loves us. And He knew that dying was the only way to save us."

"When Jesus died on the cross, He took all the wrong things anyone has ever done, like hitting, lying, stealing, or sneaking, and carried them away. Kind of like how Mr. Edwards carries all those garbage bags to the dumpster."

"Ewwww," someone muttered.

"Exactly," Eden said. "Sin is grosser than trash, but Jesus carried it anyway. He carried all our mess, all the wrong things we've done, and all our mistakes to the cross so we wouldn't have to carry it ourselves. That's how much He loves us."

"After Jesus died, they buried Jesus in a big cave. Then… one, two, three days later…He came back to life!
And He wasn't a ghost. He was really real! You could hug Him and eat fish with Him and everything."

Eden's eyes sparkled.

"It was like when a superhero falls in a movie and everyone gasps, but then BAM!, they get back up and win. Only this wasn't pretend. Jesus really came back to life. For real!"

"Then Jesus went back up to Heaven in like an invisible elevator!" Eden said, raising her hand toward the ceiling. "Well not really invisible because everyone saw Him go up to Heaven but still. Now He's the King of everything, forever."

"What's Heaven like?" a classmate asked.

"That's like the sparkliest, happiest place you could ever imagine but better." Eden answered.

"Better than Disneyland?" another classmate whispered.

Eden nodded. "Way better. Heaven doesn't run out of popcorn or close at bedtime. There's no crying, no scraped knees, and no bad times. Just perfect peace, forever."

Eden's eyes lit up as she went on, "In Heaven, the streets shine like gold. There's no sun or night because God's light is always shining. Everyone is full of joy, like the best laugh you ever had, but it never ends!"

One of Eden's classmates raised his hand and asked, "Like the biggest birthday party ever?"

"Yes!" Eden smiled. "Except it never ends, and everyone's invited."

"Can we meet Jesus and go to Heaven someday?" another classmate asked.

"Absolutely!" Eden answered. "Anyone who believes that Jesus died for our mistakes will go and be with Him in Heaven."

"That's so cool!" the classmate yelled.

"Yeah," said Eden. "And to help us while we're still on Earth, Jesus sent the Holy Spirit to live in people who believe in Him so we can be brave and kind and not scared of anything anymore. It's a gift. The best gift. Like better than money in a birthday card."

Eden's classmates' eyes grew wide. "Whoa... who's that?" they asked all at once.

Eden grinned. "Hmm... how about I bring the Holy Spirit to our next Show and Tell? He's invisible, but not pretend. You can't see the wind, but you know it's there. That's kind of how He is.""

"Yeah!" everyone cheered.

Mrs. Jenson smiled and said, "I think we'll all want to hear about that."

The class burst into claps. Some of Eden's classmates shouted, "I wanna hear more about Jesus!"

Others yelled, "Bring Him again next time too!"

Eden looked around the room and smiled.

"So that's my Show and Tell," she said. "I didn't bring a toy... I brought Jesus! But really, He's the one who brought me."

Eden's face glowed with joy. She knew this wasn't just any Show and Tell, sharing Jesus made it the best one ever.

Also available from Jude and John

The Good News of Jesus Christ presents the full gospel in clear, simple language, connecting the story of salvation from creation to the resurrection of Jesus so children gain clarity, confidence, and a strong foundation for understanding Scripture. Unlike many books that focus on Jesus as a friend or teacher, this story shows Him as He truly is: God in the flesh, the Savior of the world, and invites children to begin their walk with Christ rooted in truth and ready to share the good news. (Ages 5-12)

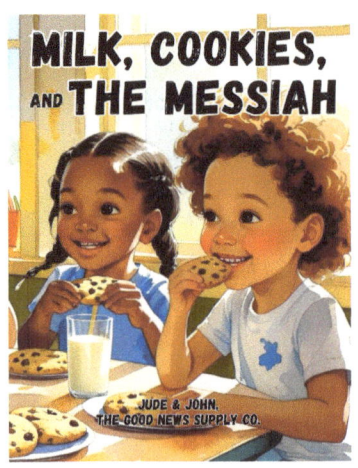

When Eden sits down for lunch, she does not expect to talk about Jesus, but soon everyone is sharing their beliefs, and Eden responds with truth from the Bible. Milk, Cookies, and The Messiah introduces children to the basics of Christian apologetics in a simple, age-appropriate way, showing them how to listen kindly, ask thoughtful questions, and stand confidently in their faith. In a world that often challenges biblical truth, this gentle story equips young readers to understand different beliefs and share God's truth with confidence. (Ages 6-12)

Jude and John, *The Good News Supply Co.*
www.JudeAndJohn.com